2⁰⁰

Milk Fever

KADDY BENYON was born in 1973 and grew up in Suffolk. She studied Literature, Life & Thought at Liverpool John Moores University and has an MA in Creative Writing from Anglia Ruskin University. She worked as a television scriptwriter prior to having children and has recently been named a *Granta* New Poet. She is currently Invited Poet at the Scott Polar Research Institute in Cambridge.

Milk Fever

by

KADDY BENYON

CROMER

PUBLISHED BY SALT PUBLISHING
12 Norwich Road, Cromer, Norfolk NR27 0AX United Kingdom

© Kaddy Benyon, 2012, 2013

The right of Kaddy Benyon to be identified as the
author of this work has been asserted by her in accordance
with Section 77 of the Copyright, Designs and Patents Act 1988.

Salt Publishing 2012, 2013

Printed and bound in the United Kingdom by Lightning Source UK Ltd

Typeset in Paperback 9 / 13

ISBN 978 1 84471 904 4 hardback
ISBN 978 1 84471 967 9 paperback

1 3 5 7 9 8 6 4 2

for Mum

There was, is, in most of us a girl-child still longing for a woman's nurture, tenderness, and approval, a woman's power exerted in our defense, a woman's smell and touch and voice, a woman's strong arms around us in moments of fear or pain.

— ADRIENNE RICH, 'Of Woman Born'

Contents

Acknowledgements

I am grateful to the editors of the following publications where some of these poems, or versions of them, first appeared: *Mslexia*; *London Magazine*; *Ambit*; *Popshot*; *Agenda* and online *Agenda Broadsheets*; *Magma*; *Granta* [online]; the *Frogmore Papers*; *Stand* and the *Cambridge News*.

'Fitzwilliam Selkie' and 'Call it Love' appeared in *A Roof of Red Tiles*, (Cinnamon Press, 2011); 'Milk Fever', 'Amongst Women' and 'In Vitro Heuresis' will appear in *Jericho*, (Cinnamon Press, 2012). A manuscript of 18 of these poems was shortlisted by Don Paterson, Jackie Kay, John Stammers and Sarah Crown for the inaugural Picador Poetry Prize 2010; 'Ice Fishing' was shortlisted by Matthew Sweeney for the Fish Poetry Prize 2010 and 'Firekeepers' came 3rd in the *Mslexia* Poetry Competition 2012, chosen by Gillian Clarke.

I wish to thank my tutor and mentor, Michael Bayley, for his humour, advice, and encyclopedic knowledge of poetry; Mary Chadwick for her orange cushion and unfailing support and the late Dr. Edmund Cusick who knew I was a poet long before I did. Thanks are also due to my fellow writers at Angles who've critiqued this collection from its inception; my friends at Anglia Ruskin University and the staff and students at the Scott Polar Research Institute in Cambridge. My gratitude goes to my friends and very noisy family, to the Dykstra family in America and to my sister, Lucy, for the weekend in Norfolk. Most importantly, thank you Chris, Libby and Thomas – without you none of this would have been possible.

Riptide

A gulch in the cliffs of Ischia,
Where a far-flung mother sparked life

From rubbed bones, worked alone
With blades of moon to carve

My pulse, my shell, the slit vessel
Of my heart. She spindled my umbilicus

From yarns of wasted babies, let the sea
Swell violence inside a crowded, silty

Caul. My birth was sudden slaughter,
A waxing scythe that tossed and heaved

Great waves peeling my limbs
Of lochia; that cloying skin of sleep.

My birth was murderous purging,
A spew to the swaddle of weeds.

Unknotted I drifted the shift of sands
And tides that tried to smother me.

Fitzwilliam Selkie

after 'Wave Spinning' 2008, by Maggi Hambling

Find a museum, a bookshop, a park
when feeling mournful, all at sea.
Sit on a bench, hold tight, invite
nobody in with words or eyes or sighs,
just be – be still in the flotsam
of crashing moods, believe in the selkie
(her silk kelp skirts and impish smile),
let her slowly surface from oil-spattered
spindrifts, loop your pale fingers
through the curves of her spine, rest
your head on her shoulder while she sails
you back to life, surfing a blue-green
vein along the estuary of your wrist.

Maman

i.m. *Louise Bourgeois*

Your veined hands slap marble
Buttocks, cup stone scrotums smooth
As eggs. You fondle a jacaranda pod

Trace its cleft as you speak of the dead
Husband, son, faithless father. The bent
spiders of your fingers work skeins

That span a near-century of rage.
You catch the watery eye of the camera
And say: *It is difficult to be a woman*

And be likeable. Beneath sapped breasts
You sigh, as though this whole grown
World is but a memory in red. A wound

Left open. A wound left open, Maman.

Cuttings

Sometimes I fear a secret camera
in your shed. Its eye on me
as I wait in that choked, cobwebby
space like a chewed toy or the sad lop

of a hooked and withered onion.
Pinch-necked poppy heads bulge
with next year's seed, beside them
your foundling, cradled snug in its pot –

just waiting for a budding. Envy
for that fleshy sprig worms into me.
I want to murder your coddled weed
yet I want to cup it and tend it,

graft your stem with mine. Give me
my own container. In its pit I will lay
our crocks, the hoard of treasures
you gave unwittingly. I will prop

each precious wedge under a knotty
heart, empty my pockets of ash.
Lend me wise gloves for the sewing
and let us bury this pip four-handed,

sink it safe between sage and apple
tree; rhododendron and pebble.

Be Prepared to Bleed

for Kate – 'If you want me I'll be in the bar.'

'Okay, fine! Have it your way', you yell
and vanish past the sad landing mirror
wondering what's become of your darling,
wide-smiled child. I see you in my tears,

hunched at the piano, an elbow propping
your grand tired head as you plink the start
of *A Case of You* slowed to a grim adagio.
I see you in my tears as I scream through

my pillow: linen, feathers, dead dreams,
finding I've descended unremembered stairs
to be back at your side, squeezed myself
next to you on the flip-lidded stool, rested

my head on your shoulder where you nuzzle
it with your cheek and unspeaking, nudge
me in the ribs with a grin as you warble
and shrill I'm in your blood like holy wine.

Pomegranate & Pin

I have waited for the tenth day
to tear this fruit apart,
my thumbs dig deep in its rusty skin,

get stung by its sharp, slick spill.
Just six of these gelled seeds –
swaddled embryos bursting with talent –

I've placed on my tongue, kept warm
as a first kiss, safe as a daughter.
Look, a globe of pale moon spins,

a darkening world turns below.
Between fair freckles of a star-blown
night and hard arthritic roots

pulsing beneath my feet, I stand alone
inside this moment, inside
this covenant I am making with you,

with her, the self I pray to find.
I push my fingers inside the two half-shells,
into unhealed flesh; live fibres

until a kind of blood weeps to my wrists,
leaks on my chest. I bury the pips
around a mountain ash, whispering

my hurts, my fears, my lusts
until the language I nursed on runs dry.
I seal my eyes, my lips, each failure

and regret as I crush the seeds, feel
a bittersweet surge of life, its prickling
rush urging me to taste, to become

and keep on becoming both
the weapon and the wound, Persephone
and Demeter; pomegranate & pin.

Strange Fruit

Sometimes I have an urge to slip
my hands inside the soiled, wilting
necks of your gardening gloves;
to let my fingers fill each dusty
burrow, then close my eyes and feel
a blush of nurture upon my skin.

Sometimes I am so afraid my hurt
will hack at your figs, strawberries,
or full-bellied beans, I dig my fists
in my pockets and nip myself. Sometimes
I imagine the man who belongs to
the hat hanging on the bright-angled

nail in your shed. I think about you
toiling and sweating with him;
coaxing growth from warm earth;
pushing life into furrows. I am curious
about what cultivates and blooms
there in your enclosed, raised bed –

yet I want no tithe of it for myself.
Sometimes I just want to show
you the places I'm mottled, rotten
and bruised; I want you to lean close
enough to hold the strange fruit
of me and tell me I may yet thrive.

Memory in Red

We picked wolf peaches in the rain,
dropped them into skirt-lips
held wide as a receiving blankets, wiped
them bright as pins and delivered

them grinning to your sun-bled kitchen.
Over half-moons you watched me
peel myself to knickers, tie myself twice
in your spare apron while preserving

jars rattled on the stove. You hauled
them out with tongs at their necks
and they wept to be swaddled and filled.
Eying your calloused fingers as you cut,

dice, drip and scrape, I find I am aching
for the mother who left me in a car
parked across two spaces, doors agape
like dislocated hips. I imagine her

hacking a path home to me, a miracle
back from the blue with unbruised eyes,
a smile so ripe, her arms unclasped
and on her cheek, a single drop of milk.

Milk Fever

You, my Inuit mother – those
low-slung cheeks, watery eyes hidden
inside a fur-lined hood, breasts you
couldn't unpack in time for your milk

to be supped unfrozen. You strapped
me to a sled, wrapped tight in pelts,
a matted fleece, some buckskin
stretched and dried that summer

you grew me inside you. A reek
of hunt and meat, a thick blood
pulsing the air with each numb thud
of your snow boots kicking up ice,

glittering my hair. North you trekked,
the sled ropes tied to your waist
as you grunted, sweat and chapped.
All I wanted was for you to stop –

hold me still a moment, not leave
me tethered to a lumber pole
as you hacked pale blue blocks, stacked
them to build a snow-dome shelter.

You lit a fire in its pit, heated meltwater
in a wide, silver bowl and held it
steaming wildly to my lips. Head dipped,
you left me in a darkness of sniffing

bear and fox, like a dream, a fear
I wake from: drifts of white linen, you
asleep nose-to-nose with me, almost
invisible, mere breath on my face.

Ice Fishing

A bear, you pound the frozen lake

creaking its lid to tipping, tackle box
lapping at your hip.

Snowblind, I follow your braille
of scratches, holler into darkness
Daddy, wait!   Daddy!

                          Then, silence
until great breaths spinning, eyes
a glitter of night you roar
at my clattering rods, disgorge
yourself from clutter, lie pelt down
listening for a clink and swirl beneath:

the scent of rotten ice.

We hack a hole, chiseling it out,
pack it with twigs and moss, leaving
a finger space for a line, a lure,
the possibility of a net.
                          Once,
you'll let me stir the socket's slush,
frustrate its surge to heal.

I'll want to scoop this negative moon
inside warm cupped hands;

tip it up, let it drip.

Night Pirate

for Colette

Tidemarks of salt
crusting his parted lips,

waxy shell nostrils;
a glassy heat in his eyes.

I hold him to me,
little one, my hallway ghost

in pirate sleepsuit:
starry-eyed, rickety-chinned;

a spill of seawater
as he dissolves unashamedly

to a wild, jagged yowl. I
cup his sopping face

and fold him into me,
curled stowaways listening

for morning in a narrow berth.
He parrots his dreams:

the *limy didor, garey monter*
like a rum-drunk sleeptalker.

I stroke, kiss, hush. He rests
a soggy hand on my arm

in case I jump ship. My
hallway ghost, my night pirate

smelling of salt water and fever;
salt water, fever and bounty.

Palm House

Your grandmother says you teetered
all day – spiked shrieks exciting
glasshouse sweat – *a feverish
temperament*, she said. I sensed
a cyclone under the lip of your wilting
hat and plucked you from a canopy of jade

vine and steamed panes to a bright, wide
lawn where you pirouetted a fountain,
limp daisies chained at your neck.
I clapped and you bowed,
frowned, then see-sawed a wet ledge,
cocking your head as you finger-dipped

to dissolve a murky twin. Now, sweetheart –
there is only this: the clack, clack
of your saccharine clock,
you rocking hot, sticking to my breast,
my tips untangling each knot
of your spine. I nuzzle your damp neck,

its fuzzy scent of roots, algae and sun,
yet your moist chest judders still,
pulses qualms into me. I trace your clammy
heartline and wish I could offer you more
than this parched and arid time
with its heat; the sweltering heat.

Holy Water (I)

Now the blessing, the readiness of Christ
be with all those who stare or fall into this river.

– ALICE OSWALD

River: a bleak seductress –
mussitating, black, beckoning.
She suggests answers under her silt,
inky veins: the tangled tributaries
that surge and curse the fens.

Step closer, teetering to a mutter
of tricked thoughts as they pulse
in reverse – whispers to wisps of light –
the somatic throb of ancient hurts.
Here is the slipping point, here

where chlorotic roots slacken to slime.
Lean over the river's mutable skin
and catch a twin reflected back –
fleetingly, lovingly; the shock of
tenderness grazing the heart like water.

Feel your head tip up, your right foot
ever so slightly lift from the earth.

Coppering

A parting shot, you called it,
the chocolate coin launched
hot from my pocket, its orange
case embossed with a crest

of rage. It makes me sick to
think of you finding the gibbous
disc, how it would have sunk
to your touch, the febrile heat

from my hip conducting to
your fingertips, seeping a dirty,
bitter stain. Did you recoil
from the token I thought cried

love? Dunk the very thought
of me until my image hissed –
then hushed – a whisper
of regret smelted in my throat:

undetonated, unutterable lump.
Perhaps your furious missive
might extract some treasure
from my rusted core, or trigger

a green crust round my heart.
Our gold's debased, its lustre
lost. Rain corrodes
the bedsprings on the dump.

Mine
or *Pachamama's Empty Nest*

My thirty-three sons never surrendered
to the dark. I sheltered them sealed
in my depths, arched a safe spine
above each precious neck, fed warm
drips in licks from bitter-tasting walls

while the gods bellyached and quaked
to break backs, conspired their worst
to plunder my veined pocket of rock.
I stayed unpenetrated and nursed
my restless babes, cradled them close

on cold stone beds as they dreamed:
sunlight on a sill, a woman tipping milk
from a terracotta jug. How the *hombres*,
earned plaudits; the hard-headed rescuers
who dared call our nest a living hell.

Well, drag them to my sunken court,
judge for yourselves who tended them
best. For here in my copper heart a lantern
burns for my stolen boys to return
some day – all of them, mine, always.

13th OCTOBER 2010

Firekeepers

She'd plait my prairie-grass hair
as though weaving a baby corn doll,

I'd close my eyes, inhale pollen, resin
and woodsmoke from her skin.

She'd say: *never let the embers sleep*
wake them up with a stick like this –

and tickle me with sooty fingers.
Winter, she left for the kindling crop,

a hand-carved hatchet on her back.
Seven pale moons have since turned

their wounded faces and some nights,
waist-deep, I part the forest seeking

the glint edge of pulsing swamp
where she swore fireflies hatch under

the curled, peeling skins of pawpaw
trees. I tiptoe in, pinch the soft eggs

between my fingertips and study
my stolen glow. I want to tap the light

forever, treasure it in a jar on the porch,
hear the rhythmic clink of light bodies

thrown like hailstones against ice. I
dream her home: armfuls of hornbeam,

larkspur and blueberries for breakfast.
Yet each new day her bunk is empty,

logs lie brittle in their pit, her lantern
on the porch a silenced heap of ash.

Los Niños

In 1999, American anthropologist Johan Reinhard, accompanied by his Argentine and Peruvian colleagues, uncovered a sacred site at 22,000 feet on Mount Llullaillaco, Argentina where three perfectly preserved Inca children had been sacrificed.

SUN VIRGIN

Sister, picked for perfection, ten
summers when the men came seeking
future wives or sacrifice. We hiked

highlands, virgin forests, plains
and jagged foothills – the luscious flanks
of the Andes – cutting a raw track

to the ridge-top site for your death
on the icy summit. Fog banks gather
in the embers of last night's

fires where we sang, toasted corn
for your final passage; prayed *Mama
Quilla* show you the way

safe from our quartered land.
Sunrise, I swathed you in *cumbi*, a headdress
of tropical feathers, set your spoon

and dishes at your side, poured
chicha into a wood cup, laid out your distaff,
your comb, tucked coca leaves

between your lips. This honour
is yours, sister – but I mourn you. Descending
chill mountain stairs alone,

a condor wheels the white
sky, a light-spear ruptures the heavens
and I know you have arrived.

BOY

He weeps for his dog and herd – yet
not his mother, brothers or kinsmen
fallen out of sight on the forty-day
horse-shoe trek up this battered
sombrero of volatile rock.
He refuses food, water, even to toy
with the gold and silver figurines
painstakingly crafted for his sacrifice.

When I look back, he is perched there
on that sacred ledge, his head dipped
on his knees, white feathers lifting
like smoke from quaking temples
as he struggles for breath, his small feet
eased from his sodden espadrilles
and tucked beneath him as if seeking
warmth, a last cinder of earthly warmth.

Lightning Girl

I am returned here to visit
        The teeth sunk-rooted
                In my one-time mouth,

Shocked apart by a flaming
        Bolt from maddened
                Intl. My body surrendered

Its soul so fast, yet,
        Generations lapsed,
                My vital organs: heart,

Spleen, still cup their blood.
        My caved cheeks
                Charred, gelid with marks

Of undead darkness
        Are now a bad omen
                For my people, my people's

People who pray me
        A benign deity. Some
                Mountain spirit sheltered

Me, let me rest in peace, rest
        Uncovered, a shrine,
                In the spine of the Andes.

The Death Collector

A vulture and a mother both, I trail
this caravan of children until their last
horizon. I swoop, curve, loop
and whirl the thermal skywaves
above these frigid peaks. Do not fear

my landing, the billowing cape of char-
black wings, I shall alight gently,
talon-down to nurse the hatching
of your deaths; the slight uncurling mists
of your shallow final breaths. Carrion,

you will never be. I may peck
at the toughest cords, sever the sinewy
strings to life, but only to free you,
children, to release your souls to fly
with me and roost with our sun-god, Inti.

My American Parents

for Carol and Ken

had a lime chenille sofa.
On it, they ate popcorn
naked, dripping in butter.

My taller father took doors
off hinges, kept a barrel
of red almonds in his shed.

He drank iced tea from a blue,
clay mug, dripped over
a spade as he dug a garden

pit where he would toast
marshmallows at night
and nuzzle my other mother.

Poem #87

I cannot count the ways, define
or describe it in a lexicon fit for kids –

yet this much I know: when I hear you
grind a pip between your teeth (a fig

seed or fleshy rag of flecked berry),
I want to share breakfast with you. I

want to see your hair fluffy, not brushed,
your clothes rumpled not pressed,

your cheeks creased and scratched
with the carvings of abstract dreams.

I want to trace your veins for a warmth
I barely recognise, to lip the blue-grey

gullies beneath your eyes, to breathe in
your neck, your chest – sunlight

and marzipan. I want to predict your body's
choreography as you reach for a pair

of home-thrown mugs, mutter *fuck*
as you burn the toast around the edges,

then grin, spreading your fingers inside my terry
robe as the coffee pot splutters, sighs.

Our Lady

I see the earthenware head, rough, crude, powerful & radiant, of dusky orange-red terracotta color, flushed with vigor and its hair heavy, electric.

– SYLVIA PLATH

My sister claimed and ruined her first.

That summer of storms and sticky scents,
my damp body budding, swollen
from the heat and jut of gawky angles

becoming domed, mossed nooks of lust
and hate. Mother pressed beatific
smiles across creased cheeks, barely

there through veils of steam, unaware
of the weapon that hissed and spat
from her sedated, blistered fist. We ran

from her kitchen to a thicket of knotted
trees where we found a terracotta
head. My sister unearthed her blank stone

eyes, kicked a hole in her crown, used
her for an ashtray, jabbing at me
when I asked for a drag. Bored, she left me

raw and alone, crawling inside a hollow
stump to cradle the fired vessel
in my skirt. I stroked its cold, porous skin

and learned to absorb rain; divulge nothing.

Holy Water (II)

You retreat as an oarswoman sculls
the river's wide turn, her blades churning
black waters that will thicken

to a nighttime slush. Her face is lit
with sweat and dread, her hair steams
in a rain that hints at a hazy corona.

She is crowned by the effort of bearing
both stern and bow, her vessel's rival tides;
the tension that tugs between desire

and loss. You watch as she hauls spray-
flecked oars from the river's ravenous drag,
glides inside a shaft of alluvial light,

to bisect a perfect symmetry of wood
and flesh quartering air. Her head dips
as if in prayer as she contemplates

knuckles blued by freezing blood, nails
split and bitten, veins swelling to a perilous,
rising tide. You urge her to warm

the font of her palms with steady, gentle
breaths, to swaddle her poor derelict hands
in her armpits, let a slow heat return.

Communion

You looked like a scuffed child-bride
of Christ, a ghost
in broderie anglaise, a new

bangle on your play-bruised wrist,
your nan's crucifix stuck
to the jam stain on your chest.

It was hot as you posed for photos:
boys pinching; girls
hissing their secret wounds.

What you remember is not
the thorn-shaped burn
on your dress, or how your dad's

glasses darkened to the sun; not
your mum's twisting fingers
or the distance between your siblings,

but the warm rasp of Sister
Aideen's voice, motes
of spit lifting from her enraptured

mouth as she swayed and sang
You Are The Gift.
How you felt met when she winked

at you; how gratefully you took her smile.

[31]

Call it Love

She asks you what it could mean
that you want to touch the blood

orange curves of her mind; that you
find yourself begging, bartering,

performing for a portion of her heart.
She says you may never know

what it is to be loved, if you can't tell
first why you smile when she trips

on words unready for speech; why
her frown makes you hurt for the soft

rock of her hips; why you are shaken
by forgetting her teeth, her lips,

the haven in her voice. You do not
know why you are afraid of the dark,

dark red of her clogs; of the bark
inside her coughs; why you want

to howl when she greets you first
on Thursdays in low sleepy vowels;

why you want to curl up inside her;
why you want to curl up, inside her.

Mummy

I.

My glamorous ancient mother.
The sacrifice of your dried lips
Parted as though the shifts
From sleep to death were nothing
But a startled dream, a
Seamless relocation of spry spirit

As your body descended
To wild, unchartered worlds
Sealed generation upon generation
Until you were disposed for us
To meet. I admire, that's not the word,
Your adorned breasts now sapped flat,
Blackened medicine pouches
Ransacked like your grave.

II.

My chamois skin desires its own tattoos,
Craves blue rivers rushing to my nipples,
Vivid clan-scars as evidence or proof
Of the Isis within. I circle you,
Charmed by your amulet, the torc,
Your carefully woven hair, how

The crockery vessels of your eyes
Flicker strange light in no-life,
How your frozen stoop seats
The primitive curve of your son's spine
(Footless foetus still in darkest peat)
His unyielding pod steeped in bitumen,
Unmolested, perfect, preserved there
Forever against bleeding, breathing: a life.

Sirius

If we long to believe that the stars rise and set for us,
that we are the reason there is a Universe,
does science do us a disservice in deflating our conceits?

– CARL SAGAN

Afterward, we took Flo to the planetarium:
the three of us reclining under a copper dome,
darkening like the linea nigra of Greenwich.
Doctor Rylance battled asteroids and tongue-tie
as he led our shpace ship shafari and Flo grinned,

clinging to sleeves and knees. The doppler
had landed hard on the atlas of my belly, roamed
the nocturnal pocket we had made. We hunted
Sirius, the bright winking of your heart
and hoped you'd refract back, send galloping news

that you lived. The sonographer turned breach,
a contortionist in her sweaty efforts to probe
new life. She discovered a suffocated astronaut
suspended in space; a dozing night watchman,
alien head dipped. No bipolar flow, no swoosh

or suck, just a dust pillar unpulsing, your clustered
limbs extinct. You'd have been our winter son,
we your shepherd moons watching you explore
this blue marble. Maybe fifty-six days was enough,
enough to complete you, dwarf planet; new star.

Cold Dark Matter

Almost as though they (the fragments) were coming back to-
gether, so you could experience the damage from a quiet place.

— CORNELIA PARKER

I packed in my seed tray
her shed and everything in it:
the fallen mud-clogged boots,
the dribbling cans of paint,
the piles of broken pots and crocks,
the leaning tower of bent hats,
the wine box on the high shelf holding
children's spades (one orange, one yellow –
its handle scuffed and grazed),
the green plastic basin filled with earth and bulbs,
the small pot of plant feed with a curling purple lid,
the spiky dried flower or dead sea thing,
the hand painted vase with five sprigs of thyme,
the dark locked cupboard I used to stroke
when sure I was utterly alone,
the squat, dusty lamp always turned on,
the chewed rubber dog toy and coiled lead,
the old fashioned push mower hanging from a rack,
the Christmas tree stand I feared
might fall on my head if I slammed the door,
all the brooms and trowels and forks,
the black buckled chair I never sat on,
the heart-cast keyring on the second hook,
the double-knotted carrier bag I dreamt
contained stones or the bones

of others who had loved her,
the dirty faded gardening gloves
moulded to the shape of her absent hands.

Among Women

This time I will not miss you.
I will not miss you because

I will not think about you,
your turquoise sweater, mother

of pearl buttons at your neck.
I will not look for you in a crowd

or wish for you to call. I will
not dream I am your daughter,

your postulant, your friend.
I will not pray for you or to you,

Blest art thou. Blessed, no –
this time I will barely notice

that you are gone, gone. This time.

Your Question

makes me blush. In the silence
between words, I imagine you naked,

brushing your teeth; pulling faces
in the rear mirror at a churlish teenage

son. I imagine you on your knees
weeding, flushed with grime and sweat,

flashing your tits at a rapt husband
as he stops to sop the heat. I imagine

you laughing, fucking, sleeping – all
unbeside me. I imagine you right here

in this room, missing me never. *I never
think about you when we're apart*, I reply.

Confession

You adore him most on Thursdays.
Rising in the still-dark, a wry
smile in your eyes as your spirit

flees our unravelled sheets. I peek
through slats of fear-stuck
sleep, sense your body's keen retreat

and wonder if this day you might spurn
me less. Wednesday nights –
you prepare for him like a lover,

faithfully scourging and anointing
by flickering flame, conjuring
him from abstinence to pull fingers

through your hair. A floor above,
I work at a vacant screen
listening to distant drips, the graze

of blades and fingers unsucking
from cream. I am exiled
from your night time rites

as you shroud yourself from touch,
rapture, loss. The waste
of your lips that now only sting,

or worship in hooded silence one
who priest-like purges memory
from memory, exorcises your dreams.

Confirmation

I had a habit of making promises
I couldn't keep, like the secret
of why Moira was late for Chemistry.
Stealing in with a boyfriend's spunk
on her sleeve she thrust it under
my nose like a receipt. *I held out
'til he said he loved me* she smirked
and guessing I may spread the word,
held my biro over a bunsen, let plastic

magma sear its stigmata on my palm.
I am scarred by the time I scorned
your kind-of prayer. Lying in a numb
dark, you experimenting with drinking
from me, eating from me, taking all
of me home to meet your parents.
You shrank when I laughed at your gasps
of love, hissed we could have been
amazing, if only I had said the words.

Body Language

Curled into you some mornings
I have no words.
My body jolts, contracts,
retracting things I've yet to say,
or feel beyond dumb memories
that stir and shake my bones

rattling to be known and spoken,
yet disowned to murky underworlds.
Often its still dark in the garden,
the room its familiar scent
of hyacinths, spent matches,
coffee we never drink – the clank

and rasp of the radiator exhaling
no warmth between us. It's your sighs
that split the silence, shrinking
me to an unutterable thought:
I am numb to the speech of bodies
and lust; I am impossible to touch.

Mummy Bare Legs

I wanted to say how lovely
you looked in your chambray skirt,
bare legs, cream linen vest.

I wanted to say your hair –
not quite tucked behind your right
ear – made me feel breakable.

I wanted to say I'd dreamt
myself adored, a child touching
your face blind-fingered

the entire nine day night.
I wanted to say maybe next time
you come home, my voice

won't leap then buckle;
disintegrate to wing-thin shadows,
a crane fly at your window.

Local History

Years from now, when you're bent
and creased, you might look up

from your piano one morning
in early May and remember a girl

who for months tried to predict
the day your pastel rhododendron

would flower. You may not recall
her voice or smell, the washed-out

skin beneath her eyes, but you'll
remember a book, there was a book,

a pale blue book with an igloo,
a cave or a shipwreck on the cover.

Perhaps you'll stroll to the library
and – no longer having her name –

weigh each title on your tongue,
run a dry finger along dust-covered

spines, pause at the gap between
Bennet and Benson feel the space

where you might have held her.

Martha

Perfect, tiny, baby girl with bruising
nails and blue-tinged skin.
Your lips, a marooned bud, darken
as we pace stunned outside the waste

of space we had created to love you.
Your father's eyes I'm sure,
we'll never see – beneath a stiff fringe,
slicked back with your mother's

efforts and all the kisses we can offer
too late. Your grandfather cradles
you inside his great bear arms,
touches your nose with a little finger,

bites his lip at the agony of losing you.
I lift you from his quaking grip
and stroke your un-chubby cheeks,
not quite cool, struggling to take in

that I will never tickle you or breathe
your milky scent; never hear you laugh
or cry. It doesn't matter that you
will never smile, still, you were born.

Holy Water (III)

She strokes me
    with the syncopated touch
        of a mother

who has lost
    her child. Each day,
        upstream and down,

the slish and sloosh
    will cease as she drifts
        back to him – dreaming

him curled tightly
    inside the empty tomb
        of her arms. She folds

herself around
    memories of nascent
        hair slick as weeds;

the knee-jerk grip
    of small curled fingers;
        the rasping bluetones

of a pulse
    that couldn't regulate;
        his skin, his marble skin.

Cradle Cap

These first dead days of January,
he curls into me, knees at my breast,
little chest juddering,

his fragile skin tugging memories
awake. Some
distant self begins to heckle

and growl, a wolverine peeking
through one slit eye, nose
lifting to the scent of danger. I sense

you in violet flickers, in the quickening
drips that fatten and spill
down the candle's unlicked

bone. I nuzzle the sparse down
on his tiny head,
inhaling his small, sour breaths

as if I could keep them. On the edge
of that frayed,
unguarded space he is almost

you, dreaming. Damp-eyed, I held
your lolling gaze
when dark cells rushed in

to multiply, copulate, reproduce
their grisly intent.
I stroke his tangy mesh of flake

and fur; of course crust and moulting
wisps that fall
to the slightest lip rub or nail tug –

I want to pick him clean: to preserve
him protected
from the ravenous urge to love.

Hairball

I envy the fucking
cat – pretty little
slink, arching back,
quivering tail, dainty
eyes, nose, toes,
how she goes
to you unbidden,
nuzzles
half-yawn, half-yowl,
makes you stop, smile,
offer your hand
while she rolls in your scent,
makes you howl

at her lithe leaps,
how she sinks claws
in your thighs,
lets you unpick her
with pleasure,
tickle her silk neck,
chuckle
as you tail-tug
through ringed fingers.
I bet you kiss
and she stretches
in the desert heat
of your desk lamp,
watching you delete mistake
                        after mistake
                                after mistake.

The Desk at Varykino

My loaded writing mule.
   Your tough legs have endured
the weight of all my dreams, and
   burdens of piled-up thoughts.

– MARINA TSVETAEVA

The winter within my childhood thaws
recollections to flickering beats. I
scrape this desk of ice and grime,
thumb-spit wood to reveal a reflection
splintering its grain: grey flesh,
cheeks sunken, cavernous eyes liquid
and afraid. I stumble from my double
image; from a comrade starved of arms,
from the roar inside my ragged guts
insisting *touch, touch, touch!*

Clumsy, numb in fingerless gloves,
I fumble inside creaking drawers
to seek dreams of pure white paper,
a slight tide of ink lilting in a bottle, blue
slush healing at its neck. I compose
like a child testing slow fearful vowels
that scratch and yowl to life, into rhyme
as sun spills the Urals and Lara returns
from hunted sleep, her light smile
breaking; her eyes wide, brimming.

The Wolves at Varykino

after Dr Zhivago

We shall inhabit a winter palace:
a place to hibernate and grow,
to veil our world in ice, snow, frozen
cobwebs hung like lace from crystal

lanterns, as though arrested
the moment of melting. We shall hide
from mutinous reds and whites,
let the sky gift us a lunation

uncovered, undiscovered, living
as man, child and wife beneath silver
domes luminous as onions in spring,
their proud necks not yet tipped.

The boom of blood-shed pounds
our looted hearts as revolution turns
this rural land to ash, smoke
fills the Urals from dawn to burning

dusk and broken homes blacken,
lives returned to dust. Our frayed
greatcoats drift the blistering
winds, baring sooted skin, stiff eyes,

starved limbs, meatless for scavenging
wolves. They savage our dreams,
scenting our muffled cries, *The Tsar
is dead! The Tsar is dead, who will love*

us now? They bay under barbed
and fruitless trees ancient with rime
and frost, screaming like trains
through the mountains billowing hot,

insistent breaths. They circle your mind
at twilight as you hiss and shoo
and wheeze, flail wasting arms
at biting air, fall faintly to your knees.

Ice Recital

Hold the sustain pedal down,
make this note last until it's drowned.

– KATHRYN WILLIAMS

Girl in a night blue coat fuddles
a riddle of keys,
      waves as she turns into darkness,

blusters through clinking trees.
Feel your chest
      burn at the spot where she stops –

sinks in the snow-muted banks.
Picture her in polished
      satin, her mother's freshwater pearls

perhaps. Do not disturb her
as she tips the river's
      slim lid to plink its black and iced bones,

fingers quavering like frost-stilled
leaves unfurling chill,
      uncertain notes that grow in time

to pulse wildly like newborn fontanelles.
Gasp at her arms gaping wide,
      thrown at the moon; the liquid moon.

Ever After

for the Miss L.E.s

Pretty as glass, let her hold it and see it;
keep those timid gap-toothed smiles
unsmudged by disenchantment. I pray

faith in *Ever After* lets her feel me always
looking and looking and looking
as though through a chink as she skips

and claps, gasps and slides to land laughing,
grasping for a secret place to store
her childhood treasures. I ask for more

days just like these, where delight spindles
pride as she finds a friend's lost shoe,
pulls up his downturned smile, squeezes

his knee and coos: *don't cry, you're okay,
I'm here*. Little mother, my pocket
mirror curiously uncracked. Grant us

that world between seeking and knowing,
a dreamtime or an opening of auras
to enact together her drama of being six.

Camera Obscura

Your first ever camera –
like looking through the keyhole
of the darkened room

while your mother slept
coiled, her grey eyes shuttered
and stuck. You crept

into the distance of wanting
her, took shots
from every angle:

a curve of shoulder, five
curled toes, a quiver
of ribs snapped between birdsong

and silence. Reels later,
developing the negatives uncovered
at her death, you hang slivers

of silver film under a bare,
red bulb, squint in the dim light
to catch a glimpse

of one palm trapped between
her knees, the other spread-eagled
on your father's empty pillow.

Again

I'll stroke the worn creases
of your chair one last time,
the right armrest more than the left

where you would fret and unpick
the silences. I'll inhale your books,
your curios, your glasses case

snapped open and never closed.
I'll crouch to touch the orange-red
threading of your rug, rest

my finger pads in its dints
(there and there and there), rise
to see the spectacle of my many selves

reflected in the tiny, curious mirrors
stitched to your wall hanging,
lean close enough to catch

a sudden, guilty grin, knowing
this having contains a losing;
the pain of loss become a simple gain.

Mother as a Windmill

My root drills a sludge-coloured
sea, arms trisecting air,
dragging deliberate blades
to earn my offshore gruel.
I am one in a herd of turbines
reaping invisible power, a ticking
crucifixion, your skeleton
reflection in an estuary that spills
eels into copper marshlands.
Listen –

        curlews in the rushes,
beaks turned from the steel freaks
that barb a smudged horizon.
I want you: the shape of embrace,
great starfish rigged in samphire
light. If I could unsuck
from this mulching bed, hide inside
your clapboard skirt, watch oil
drip on the grind of teething cogs;
if I could unplug this swell of silt
and spume that gathers a birthmark
tar, I would stay grey-boned
and anchored, loving you cartwheel
the sky, harvest your distant
smile for my own slow return.

Holy Water (IV)

Even the river recoils as I sink
on this damp bank without you,
mother. A girl chases a dog,
tongue first and panting, a lone
oarsman pounds his spluttering
course, a lollop of fish
sucks gossamer into spirals;
into vortices gaping like mouths.
A knotted rope swings from a neck
of overhung birch, reeds and wild
flowers deny their murky roots,
a pintail ducks the water's skin
as punters coast laughter, drag lazy
fingers through pennywort,
jewelweed, rushes. A breeze unsettles
the meadow, a sag of cow-skin tightens
to hammock organs above grass
as the dung-crusted tail lashes flies.
I flinch at a mock of bird-loaded
branches; at the titter of water
rats, the rain. I hide under covers
of moss, stones and scraped, spangled
scales until a kayak slits the water,
in it a woman twice your age, white
hair spilling from a fisherman's
hat, arms moving like pistons, her
grunting chest, her steaming breath.

Loveblind Fool

Stumble unsighting
this wild, wild heath where a sulphurous
rage whitens our crown to ash

and bleak winds blow a dark-eyed
night of invisible fiends
coiling us to our knees. Uncompassed –

lurch through weeds of memory,
forked naked animals
biting at holy cords until free to feel

what only wretches feel: this cracked
and troubled solitude;
this thundering need to be loved

undivided for what we are, not what we
ought to be. Somewhere
in my deepest nature I have slenderly

known myself, groping like a blind child
or beggar, like a foolish,
fond old man seeking those endearments

from my daughters. I did you wrong
to test what was given smilingly,
dutifully (no more and no less). Forgive

the sharp-toothed unkindness that ripened
on my lips. I am naught
but an old, unhappy traitor with a heart

that pants madly for life, for bliss, to sing
a bird in a cage – for now I see
nothing – but the evidence of you, love.

Idol

The saints won't give me your face
back exactly as I like it, love

it actually, the way you think frowning,
point steepled fingers at your lips

as though praying for a flock of words;
the way you pull at your earlobes

when thoughts aren't ready for talk;
the way your abiding smile

can raise me from a cave of silence.
You've never said it in words –

those three or any others – and it isn't
in embrace or gifts or praise,

but in how you shift your subtle body
to mirror mine; in how you hold

me within the mysteries of your voice;
in how your eyes brighten

or fill with my image sometimes
when we part; in how you give

me time and time again
to contemplate the proof of your love.

In Vitro Heuresis

Let us go then to ancient Athens
and celebrate the mystery

of our purposeful design. You,
me, consciously conceived

that I may live, love, survive.
Let's play gods, you and I –

the blood music beats,
the stone moon retreats –

reap the lonely cell of me
from inside this sea of rains.

Let's nestle through the night,
incubate and contemplate

my waning thirst for birth;
sly poke each doubling

and sluggish doubling,
the uncoupling of my halves.

You are my secret, surrogate
other nursing a soul at dawn,

each knock and bump and nub
of me, bit-by-bit becoming

a kicking wee homunculus
front-crawling to the lip

of a petrified world to emerge
noisy, hungry, woman, whole.

Bumble Boy

The summer your father became a distant
drone, I dozed under a veil of blossom, felt

the first pulse of you under a blizzard of bees
fanning to cool their heavy-egged queen.

You fattened on a time of famine; of rime
and icicles hot as stings and I slept while sticky

hormones hatched from egg, to larva to pupa.
You were an antidote to the waxwork son

who never rose: a curled, still worm sunk
in royal jelly. Yet you floated and swam

in my syrupy liquor, a bobber of tides kicking
my navel to a stamen. You rendered me

unable to fly, colonised my dreams, silenced
my needs until they smoked you out, leaving

you honey-drunk and hazy. The midwife caught
you and cut you off, hung you from a hook

to weigh each fuzz and bur of looped flesh
my sweet harvest, straining through muslin.

Easter

You're watching *Fantastic Mr Fox*, trapped
between our fidgety children.
your left fist stiff as though it's dripped
from your stalactite arm; hardened
to a cold stone knot on your lap. Our

little girl tries to scale you, smack your face
with sticky kisses but you push her
away, afraid she'll burrow right inside;
yell my name by mistake. She sulks until
I waggle a finger that hooks out a smile. Then

I am back in the fields with Daddy, after the tilt
of the mirror that winked a rear-view grin.
We left the car in trees, walked for miles,
mud sucking at our boots. He strode ahead,
binoculars swinging, then stopped

suddenly to track a kestrel pinned to the sky.
I scurried into his shadow, damp socks rucked
squinted into orbit for what had snared his
sight. Bored, I squelched off to forage
pennywort, sorrel or violets but found

a strung hare instead. It's hind legs wire-bound,
jaws cloven, rust-stained teeth broken,
whiskers and pelt ripped apart. Now I bite
into the chocolate leveret you gave me;
feel its guts melt as they slip down my throat.

Undone

We had to run for the bus after confession,
where waiting for Mother's silence
I'd made imaginary idols of saints, illuminated

by twenty votives I paid for with flickers
of prayer. We'd no time for my litany
of lies and spite and rage so the priest winked

and told me *Next time.* I reached for Mother's
hand, already crammed with beads
clacking together: a metronome for OCD.

Her illness worshipped muttering; stations
of the cross mostly, but then anything
with a repeating pattern, lost in a hail of Marys.

She let me sit by the window, while, head
bowed she vowed to settle breaths above
the throb and grind of engine. Her hands knitted

together then apart, twisting and fidgeting inside
deliberate sleeves. She looked as odd
as the panting man in the soiled mac, uncurtaining

bushes when we stopped at lights. He grinned
up at me, presenting his puffy, purpley
grub. I covered up my eyes and whispered:

How soon is next time Mummy?   Mum?

(Not) Penelope's Web

The shroud itself became a story almost instantly. 'Penelope's web,' it was called; people used to say that of any task that remained mysteriously unfinished.

– MARGARET ATWOOD, 'The Penelopead'

The expression of my creativity as a woman can feel like an expression of disobedience and, sometimes, also a destructive act.

– JULIET MILLER, 'Creative Feminine and Her Discontents'

I DO

Our first night entwined in the tree
of his living bed, he lifts silver-scaled
veils from my eyes, lands me gasping
across the threshold of desire, licks my
lips, my neck, the salt gully between
my breasts. He feasts until my spine
arches like a hunter's bow, then stops –
lifts his head, wants to swap stories
instead. Slackened, I sigh, describe
a mother more iced fish than woman;
the father who slung me out to sea;
how I lived to have my hands touched
against spiders' webs to net the craft
of creation inside the loom of my body.

I UNDO

Enchanted he pulls me on top, this time
not stopping, *please don't stop* . . .
We lock fingers and lips, tease out
the weave of our hips until I'm spinning
a son from earthcords he's rooted
inside me. My body learns bliss, *this
is surely bliss. Bliss* –

                    yet he'll leave me
solitary on this goat-strewn rock,
lured to war across a wine-blood sea,
whispered lost to goddess Calypso.
I'll be untouched when the suitors come,
their arrows nocked to snag my queendom,
my treasure, the seascape between my thighs.

I REDO

At first I still felt the weft of our fingers,
a raft in the dragtides tugging
him home. Nights I'd thrash, scream

for him, dreams frayed by hurt, rage and loss.
She's come undone the suitors mocked,
so I punished with spider-like frenzy, spun

a yarn so long they lost the thread, left me
stitchpicking my secret dark.
Finally alone, blissfully alone, after all

faithful waiting, wanting, grieving – days
spent gazing the horizons . . . the oddity
of his ship coming in made my love a many-

tentacled thing. I took him to the tangled
nest of our bed, then reader, I devoured him.

Lightning Source UK Ltd.
Milton Keynes UK
UKOW05f0826180913

217426UK00005B/16/P